CORNISH FOLK-LORE

ROBERT HUNT

TOR MARK PRESS · PENRYN

Reprinted 1988

Copyright © 1988 Tor Mark Press

ISBN 0 85025 305 5

Cover: Chun Tor Copyright © Ian Cooke
Men-an-Tol Studio

Published by
Tor Mark Press
Islington Wharf, Penryn, Cornwall TR10 8AT

Printed by
Earles Press, Station Hill, Redruth, Cornwall TR15 2AX

THE MERMAID'S ROCK

To the westward of the beautiful Cove of Lemorna is a rock which has through all time borne the above name. I have never been enabled to learn any special story in connection with this rock. There exists the popular fancy of a lady showing herself here previous to a storm—with, of course, the invariable comb and glass. She is said to have been heard singing most plaintively before a wreck, and that, all along the shore, the spirits have echoed her in low moaning voices. Young men are said to have swam off to the rock, lured by the songs which they heard, but they have never returned. Have we not in this a dim shadow of the story of the Sirens?

THE SANDS AT LELANT AND PHILLACK

There is a tradition that Lelant and Phillack towns were all meadow land, and that the whole was covered with sand in a single night. Also that the low tract of land extended on both sides of Hayle far beyond the present bar, so that the sea has swallowed up some hundreds of acres. The people say that the sight of the ancient church and village of Lelant was somewhere seaward of the Black Rock;—the ancient burial-ground has been long washed away,—and that human teeth are still frequently found on the shore after a great *undertoe*, that takes the sand out to sea. Many circumstances seem to confirm the probability of the tradition. The sand was drifting inland at such a rate before the reed-like plant called by the present inhabitants *the spire* was planted, that the whole of the land about the village would have been rendered worthless ere this, but for the stability given to it. The land from which the sand has been cleared, on the sea side of the church, has evidently been ploughed, as the furrows are quite apparent between the ridges. They say that there was a market held in Lelant when St Ives was scarcely a village. Lelant being the mother church, would seem to prove this. One can easily understand how a large tract of land of the nature of that under Lelant sand-hills would be washed away in a comparatively short time, as the soil at the low-water level is a marly clay. This is constantly being washed down by high tides, and carried away by the undercurrent, as it contains no stone to form a pebbly beach, and therefore there is nothing left to protect the shore.

THE LOST CHILD

IN THE little hamlet of Treonike, in the parish of St Allen, has long lingered the story of a lost child, who was subsequently found. All the stories agree in referring the abduction of the child to supernatural agency, and in some cases it is referred to the "Small People or Piskies,"—in others, to less amiable spiritual creatures. Mr Hals has given one version of this story, which differs in some respects from the tale as I heard it, from an old woman some thirty years since, who then lived in this parish. Her tale was to the following effect. It was a lovely evening, and the little boy was gathering flowers in the fields, near a wood. The child was charmed by hearing some beautiful music, which he at first mistook for the song of birds; but, being a sharp boy, he was not long deceived, and he went towards the wood to ascertain from whence the melodious sounds came. When he reached the verge of the wood, the music was of so exquisite a character, that he was compelled to follow the sound, which appeared to travel before him. Lured in this way, the boy penetrated to the dark centre of the grove, and here, meeting with some difficulties, owing to the thick growth of underwood, he paused and began to think of returning. The music, however, became more ravishing than before, and some invisible being appeared to crush down all the low and tangled plants, thus forming for him a passage, over which he passed without any difficulty.

At length he found himself on the edge of a small lake, and, greatly to his astonishment, the darkness of night was around him, but the heavens were thick with stars. The music ceased, and, wearied with his wanderings, the boy fell asleep on a bed of ferns. He related, on his restoration to his parents, that he was taken by a beautiful lady through palaces of the most gorgeous description. Pillars of glass supported arches which glistened with every colour, and these were hung with crystals far exceeding anything which were ever seen in the caverns of a Cornish mine. It is, however, stated that many days passed away before the child was found by his friends, and that at length he was discovered, one lovely morning, sleeping on the bed of ferns, on which he was supposed to have fallen asleep on the first adventurous evening. There was no reason given by the narrator why the boy was "spirited away" in the first instance, or why he was returned. Her impression was, that some sprites, pleased with the child's innocence and beauty, had entranced him. That when asleep he had been carried through the waters to the fairy abodes beneath them; and she felt assured that a child so treated would be kept under the especial guardianship of the sprites for ever afterwards. Of this, however, tradition leaves us in ignorance.

THE SPRIGGANS OF TRENCROM HILL

IT IS NOT many years since a man, who thought he was fully informed as to the spot in which a crock of the giant's gold was buried, proceeded on one fine moonlight night to this enchanted hill, and with spade and pick commenced his search. He proceeded for some time without interruption, and it became evident to him that the treasure was not far off. The sky was rapidly covered with the darkest clouds, shutting out the brilliant light of the moon—which had previously gemmed each cairn—and leaving the gold-seeker in total and unearthly darkness. The wind rose, and roared terrifically amidst the rocks; but this was soon drowned amidst the fearful crashes of thunder, which followed in quick succession the flashes of lightning. By its light the man perceived that the spriggans were coming out in swarms from all the rocks. They were in countless numbers; and although they were small at first, they rapidly increased in size, until eventually they assumed an almost giant form, looking all the while, as he afterwards said, "as ugly as if they would eat him." How, this poor man escaped is unknown, but he is said to have been so frightened that he took to his bed, and was not able to work for a long time.

THE SMALL PEOPLE'S GARDENS

IF THE adventurous traveller who visits the Land's End district will go down as far as he can on the south-west side of the Logan Rock Cairn, and look over, he will see, in little sheltered places between the cairns, close down the water's edge, beautifully green spots, with here and there some ferns and cliff-pinks. These are the gardens of the Small People, or, as they are called by the natives, Small Folk. They are beautiful little creatures, who appear to pass a life of constant enjoyment amongst their own favourite flowers. They are harmless; and if man does not meddle with them when they are holding their fairs—which are indeed high festivals—the Small Folk never interfere with man or anything belonging to him. They are known to do much good, especially when they discover a case of oppressed poverty; but they do it their own way. They love to do good for its own sake, and the publication of it in any way draws down their censure, and sometimes severe anger, on the object whom it was their purpose to serve. To prove that those lovely little creatures are no dream, I may quote the words of a native of St Levan:—

"As I was saying, when I have been to sea close under the cliffs, of a fine summer's night, I have heard the sweetest of music, and seen hundreds of little lights moving about amongst what looked like flowers. Ay! and they are flowers too, for you may smell the sweet scent far out at sea. Indeed, I have heard many of the old men say, that they have smelt the sweet perfume, and heard the music from the fairy gardens of the Castle, when more than a mile from the shore." Strangely enough, you can find no flowers but the sea-pinks in these lovely green places by day, yet they have been described by those who have seen them in the midsummer moonlight as being covered with flowers of every colour, all of them far more brilliant than any blossoms seen in any mortal garden.

NURSING A FAIRY

A THRIFTY housewife lived on one of the hills between Zennor Church-town and St Ives. One night a gentleman came to her cottage, and told her he had marked her cleanliness and her care: that he had a child whom he desired to have brought up with much tenderness, and he had fixed on her. She should be very handsomely rewarded for her trouble, and he showed her a considerable quantity of golden coin. Well, she agreed, and away she went with the gentleman to fetch this child. When they came to the side of Zennor hill, the gentleman told the woman he must blindfold her, and she, good, easy soul, having heard of such things, fancied this was some rich man's child, and that the residence of its mother was not to be known, so she gave herself great credit for cunning in quietly submitting. They walked on some considerable distance. When they stopped the handkerchief was taken from her eyes, and she found herself in a magnificent room, with a table spread with the most expensive luxuries, in the way of game, fruits, and wines. She was told to eat, and she did so with some awkwardness, and not a little trembling. She was surprised that so large a feast should have been spread for so small a party,—only herself and the master. At last, having enjoyed luxuries such as she never tasted before or since, a silver bell was rung, and a troop of servants came in, bearing a cot covered with satin, in which was sleeping the most beautiful babe that human eyes ever gazed on. She was told this child was to be committed to her charge; she should not want for anything; but she was to obey certain laws. She was not to teach the child the Lord's Prayer; she was not to wash it after sundown; she was to bathe it every morning in water, which she would find in a white ewer placed in the child's room: this was not to be touched by any one but herself, and she was to be careful not to wash her own face in this water. In all other respects she was to treat the child as one of her own children. The woman was blinded again, and the child having been placed in her arms, away she trudged, guided by the mysterious father. When out on the road, the bandage was removed from her eyes, and she found she had a small baby in her arms, not remarkably good-looking, with very sharp, piercing eyes, and but ordinarily dressed. However, a bargain is a bargain; so she resolved to make the best of it, and she presented the babe to her husband, telling him so much of the story as she thought it prudent to trust him with. For years the child was with this couple. They never wanted for anything; meat, and even wines, were provided,—as most people thought,—by wishing for them; clothes, ready-made, were on the child's bed when required; and the charmed water was always in the magic ewer. The little boy grew active and strong. He was remarkably wild, yet very tractable, and he appeared to have a real regard for his "big mammy," as he called the woman. Sometimes she thought the child was mad. He would run, and leap, and scream, as though he were playing with scores of boys, when no soul was near him. The woman had never seen the father since the child had been with them; but ever and anon, money was conveyed to them in some mysterious manner. One morning, when washing the boy, this good woman, who had often observed how bright the water made the face of the child, was tempted to try if it would improve her own beauty. So directing the boy's attention to some birds singing in a tree outside the windows, she splashed some of the water up into her face. Most of it went into her eye. She closed it instinctively, and upon opening it, she saw a number of little people gathered round her and playing with the boy. She said not a word, though her fear was great; and she continued to see the world of small people surrounding the world of ordinary men and women, being with them, but not of them. She now knew who the boy's playmates were and she often wished to speak to the beautiful creatures of the invisible world who were his real companions; but she was discreet and kept silence.

Curious robberies had been from time to time committed in St Ives market, and although the most careful watch had been kept, the things disappeared, and no thief detected. One day our good housewife was at the market, and to her surprise she saw the father of her nursling. Without ceremony she ran up to him,—at a moment when he was putting some choice fruit by stealth into his pocket,—and spoke to him. "So, thou seest me, dost thou?" "To be sure I do, and know 'ee too," replied the woman. "Shut this eye," putting his finger on her left eye. "Canst see me now?" "Yes, I tell 'ee, and know 'ee too," again said the woman.

> "Water for elf, not water for self;
> "You've lost your eye, your child, and yourself"

said the gentleman. From that hour she was blind in the right eye. When she got home the boy was gone. She grieved sadly, but she never saw him more, and this once happy couple became poor and wretched.

THE FAIRY TOOLS; OR, BARKER'S KNEE

THE BUCCAS or knockers are believed to inhabit the rocks, caves, adits, and wells of Cornwall. In the parish of Towednack there was a well where those industrious small people might every day be heard busy at their labours—digging with pickaxe and shovel. I said, every day. No; on Christmas-day—on the Jews' Sabbath—on Easter-day—and on All-Saints' day—no work was done. Why our little friends held those days in reverence has never been told me. Any one, by placing his ear on the ground at the mouth of this well, could distinctly hear the little people at work.

There lived in the neighbourhood a great, hulking fellow, who would rather do anything than work, and who refused to believe anything he heard. He had been told of the Fairy Well—he said it was "all a dream". But since the good people around him reiterated their belief in the fairies of the well, he said he'd find it all out. So day after day, Barker—that was this hulk's name— would lie down amidst the ferns growing around the mouth of the well, and, basking in the sunshine, listen and watch. He soon heard pick and shovel, and chit-chat, and merry laughter. Well, "he'd see the out of all this," he told his neighbours. Day after day, and week after week, this fellow was at his post. Nothing resulted from his watching. At last he learned to distinguish the words used by the busy workers. He discovered that each set of labourers worked eight hours, and that, on leaving, they hid their tools. They made no secret of this; and one evening he heard one say, he should place his tools in a cleft in the rock; another, that he should put his under the ferns; and another said, he should leave his tools on *Barker's knee*. He started on hearing his own name. At that moment a heavy weight fell on the man's knee; he felt excessive pain, and roared to have the cursed things taken away. His cries were answered by laughter. To the day of his death Barker had a stiff knee; he was laughed at by all the parish; and "Barker's knee" became a proverb.

THE FOUR-LEAVED CLOVER

NOT MANY YEARS since a farmer lived at Bosfrancan in St Burrien, who had a very fine red-and-white cow called Daisey. The cow was always fat, with her dewlaps and udder sweeping the grass. Daisey held her milk from calf to calf; had an udder like a bucket, yet she would never yield more than a gallon or so of milk, when one might plainly see that she had still at least two gallons more in her udder. All at once, when the milk was in full flow, she would give a gentle bleat, *cock up* her ears, and the milk would stop at once. If the milkmaid tried to get any more from her after that, she would up foot, kick the bucket, and spill all the milk, yet stand as still as a stock, and keep chewing her cud all the time. Everybody would have thought the cow bewitched, if she hadn't been always fat and held her milk all the year round; besides, everything prospered with the farmer, and all the other cows had more milk than any of the neighbours'. No one could tell what the deuce could be the matter with Daisey; and they tried to drive her to Burrien Church-town fair, that they might be rid of her, as she was always fit for the butchers. All the men and boys on the farm couldn't get her to Church-town. As fast as they drove her up Alsie Lane, she would take down Cotneywilley, through by the Crean, down the Bottoms, and up the Gilley, and be in the field again before the men and boys would be half way home.

One midsummer's day in the evening, the maid was later than usual milking, as she had been down to Penberth to the *games*. The stars were beginning to blink when she finished her task. Daisey was the last cow milked, and the bucket was so full she could scarcely lift it to her head. Before rising from the milking stool, the maid plucked up a handful of grass and clover to put in the head of her hat, that she might carry the bucket the steadier. She had no sooner placed the hat on her head, than she saw hundreds and thousands of Small People swarming in all directions about the cow, and dipping their hands into the milk, taking it out on the clover blossoms and sucking them. The grass and clover, all in blossom, reached to the cow's belly. Hundreds of the little creatures ran up the long grass and clover stems, with buttercups, lady's smocks, convolvuluses, and foxglove flowers, to catch the milk that Daisey let flow from her four teats, like a shower, among them. Right under the cow's udder the maid saw one much larger than the others lying on his back, with his heels cocked up to the cow's belly. She knew he must be a Piskie, because he was laughing, with his mouth open from ear to ear. The little ones were running up and down his legs, filling their cups, and emptying them into the Piskie's mouth. Hundreds of others were on Daisey's back, scratching her rump, and tickling her round the horns and behind the ears. Others were smoothing down every hair of her shining coat into place.

The cows were in the field called Park-an-Ventan, close under the house. Her mistress came out into the garden between the field and the house, and called to know what was keeping the maid so long. When the maid told what she had seen, her mistress said she couldn't believe her unless she had found a four-leaved grass. Then the maid thought of the handful of grass in the head of her hat. In looking it over by the candlelight, she found a bunch of three-leaved grass, and one stem with four leaves. They knew that it was nothing strange that she should see the Small People, but they didn't know what plan to take to get rid of them, so that they might have the whole of Daisey's milk, till the mistress told her mother about it. Her mother was a very notable old dame, who lived in Church-town. The old woman knew all about witches, fairies, and such things; was noted for being a sharp, careful old body; for when she happened to break the eye of her stocking darning-needle, she would take it to the blacksmith that he might put a new eye to it. The smith always charged her twopence. She would rather pay that than throw it away.

Our Betty told her daughter that everybody knowed that the Small People couldn't abide the smell of fish, nor the savour of salt or grease; and advised her to rub the cow's udder with fish brine to drive the Small People away. Well, she did what her mammy told her to do. Better she had let it alone. From that time Daisey would yield all her milk, but she hadn't the half, nor quarter, so much as before, but took up her udder, so that one could hardly see it below her flanks. Every evening, as soon as the stars began to twinkle, the cow would go round the fields bleating and crying as if she had lost her calf; she became hairpitched, and pined away to skin and bone before the next Burrien fair, when she was driven to Church-town and sold for next to nothing. I don't know what became of her afterwards; but nothing throve with the farmer, after his wife had driven the Small People away, as it did before.

THE OLD WOMAN WHO TURNED HER SHIFT

IN A LONE house—situated not far from the hill on which now stands Knill's Steeple, as it is called—which was then known as Chyanwheal, or the *House on the Mine*, lived a lone woman, the widow of a miner, said to have been killed in one of the very ancient "coffens," as the open mine-workings existing in this hill are termed. A village now bears this name, but it has derived it from this lone house. Whether it was that they presumed upon her solitude, or whether the old lady had given them some inducement, is not now known, but the spriggans of Trencrom Hill were in the habit of meeting almost every night in her cottage to divide their plunder. The old woman usually slept, or at least she pretended to sleep, during the visit of the spriggans. When they left, they always placed a small coin on the table by her bedside, and with this indeed the old woman was enabled to provide herself with not merely the necessaries of life, but to add thereto a few of those things which were luxuries to one in her position. The old lady, however, was not satisfied with this. She resolved to bide her time, and when the spriggans had an unusually large amount of plunder, to make herself rich at once and for ever at their expense. Such a time at last arrived. The spriggans had gathered, we know not how much valuable gold and jewellery. It gleamed and glistened on the floor, and the old woman in bed looked on with a most covetous eye. After a while, it appears, the spriggans were not able to settle the question of division with their usual amicability. The little thieves began to quarrel among themselves.

Now, thought the old woman, is my time. Therefore huddling herself up under the bedclothes, she very adroitly contrived to turn her shift, and having completed the unfailing charm, she jumped from her bed, placed her hand on a gold cup, and claimed, "Thee shusn't hae one on 'em!"

In affright the spriggans all scampered away, leaving their stolen treasure behind them. The last and boldest of the spriggans, however, swept his hand over the old woman's only garment as he left the house. The old woman, now wealthy, removed in a little time from Chyanwheal to St Ives, and, to the surprise of every one, purchased property and lived like a gentlewoman. Whenever, however, she put on the shift which had secured her her wealth, she was tortured beyond endurance. The doctors and all the learned people used hard names to describe her pains, but the wise women knew all along that they came of the spriggans.

HOW ST PIRAN REACHED CORNWALL

GOOD MEN are frequently persecuted by those whom they have benefited the most. The righteous Piran had, by virtue of his sanctity, been enabled to feed ten Irish kings and their armies for ten days together with three cows. He brought to life by his prayers the dogs which had been killed while hunting the elk and the boar, and even restored to existence many of the warriors who had fallen on the battle-field. Notwithstanding this, and his incomparable goodness, some of these kings condemned him to be cast off a precipice into the sea, with a millstone around his neck.

On a boisterous day, a crowd of the lawless Irish assembled on the brow of a beetling cliff, with Piran in chains. By great labour they had rolled a huge millstone to the top of the hill, and Piran was chained to it. At a signal from one of the kings, the stone and the saint were rolled to the edge of, and suddenly over, the cliff into the Atlantic. The winds were blowing temptestuously, the heavens were dark with clouds, and the waves white with crested foam. No sooner was Piran and the millstone launched into space, than the sun shone out brightly, casting the full lustre of its beams on the holy man, who sat tranquilly on the descending stone. The winds died away, and the waves became smooth as a mirror. The moment the millstone touched the water, hundreds were converted to Christianity who saw this miracle. St Piran floated on safely to Cornwall; he landed on the 5th of March on the sands which bear his name. He lived amongst the Cornish men until he attained the age of 206 years.

ORDULPH THE GIANT

THIS *Tavistock* Sampson, is far removed from our fine old legendary giant; yet we perceive in the stories of Ordulph precisely the same process as that which has given immortality to Blunderbuss and others. In the church of the monastery of Tavistock, built by Orgar in 960, and consecrated by St Rumon, was buried Orgar, and also his son Edulf, or Ordulph, to whom, by some writers, the foundation of the abbey is attributed. Ordulph was a man of giant size, and possessing most remarkable strength. He once appeared before the gates of the city of Exeter in company with King Edward, and demanded admission. His demand was not immediately complied with. He tore away the bars of the portcullis with his hands—burst open the gates with his foot—rent the locks and bolts asunder—and broke down a considerable portion of the wall—walking into the city over the ruins, and occasioning great alarm amidst the inhabitants.

The king is said to have attributed this extraordinary feat of strength to the chieftain's having entered into a compact with the devil; and the people generally believed the king to be correct.

At Tavistock, it was the custom of Ordulph to stand with one foot on either side of the Tavy, which is about twenty feet wide, and having the wild beasts driven in from the Dartmoor forests, he would—with the seemingly insignificant blows of a small knife—strike their heads off into the stream.

THE GIANT OF ST MICHAEL'S MOUNT LOSES HIS WIFE

THE GIANT on the Mount and the giant on Trecrobben Hill were very friendly. They had only one cobbling-hammer between them, which they would throw from one to the other, as either required it. One day the giant on the Mount wanted the hammer in a great hurry, so he shouted, "Holloa, up there! Trecrobben, throw us down the hammer, woost a'?"

"To be sure," sings out Trecrobben; "here! look out, and catch 'm."

Now, nothing would do but the giant's wife, who was very near-sighted, must run out of her cave to see Trecrobben throw the hammer. She had no hat on; and coming at once out into the light, she could not distinguish objects. Consequently, she did not see the hammer coming through the air, and received it between her eyes. The force with which it was flung was so great that the massive bone of the forehead of the giantess was crushed, and she fell dead at the giant's feet. You may be sure there was a great to-do between the two giants. They sat wailing over the dead body, and with their sighs they produced a tempest. These were unavailing to restore the old lady, and all they had to do was to bury her. Some say they lifted the Chapel Rock and put her under it, others, that she is buried beneath the castle court, while some—no doubt the giants' detractors—declare that they rolled the body down into the sea, and took no more heed of it.

THE OLD MAN OF CURY

MORE THAN A hundred years since, on a fine summer day, when the sun shone brilliantly from a cloudless sky, an old man from the parish of Cury, or, as it was called in olden time, Corantyn, was walking on the sands in one of the coves near the Lizard Point. The old man was meditating, or at least he was walking onward, either thinking deeply, or not thinking at all—that is, he was "lost in thought"—when suddenly he came upon a rock on which was sitting a beautiful girl with fair hair, so long that it covered her entire person. On the in-shore side of the rock was a pool of the most transparent water, which had been left by the receding tide in the sandy hollow the waters had scooped out. This young creature was so absorbed in her occupation,—arranging her hair in the watery mirror, or in admiration of her own lovely face, that she was unconscious of an intruder.

The old man stood looking at her for some time ere he made up his mind how to act. At length he resolved to speak to the maiden. "What cheer, young one?" he said, "what art thee doing there by thyself, then, this time o' day?" As soon as she heard the voice, she slid off the rock entirely under the water. The old man could not tell what to make of it. He thought the girl would drown herself, so he ran on to the rock to render her assistance, conceiving that in her fright at being found naked by a man she had fallen into the pool, and possibly it was deep enough to drown her. He looked into the water, and, sure enough, he could make out the head and shoulders of a woman, and long hair floating like fine sea-weeds all over the pond, hiding what appeared to him to be a fish's tail. He could not, however, see anything distinctly, owing to the abundance of hair floating around the figure. The old man had heard of mermaids from the fishermen of Gunwalloe; so he conceived this lady must be one, and he was at first very much frightened. He saw that the young lady was quite as much terrified as he was, and that, from shame or fear, she endeavoured to hide herself in the crevices of the rock, and bury herself under the sea-weeds.

Summoning courage, at last the old man addressed her, "Don't 'e be afraid, my dear. You needn't mind me. I wouldn't do ye any harm. I'm an old man, and wouldn't hurt ye any more than your grandfather."

After he had talked in this soothing strain for some time, the young lady took courage, and raised her head above the water. She was crying bitterly, and, as soon as she could speak, she begged the old man to go away.

"I must know, my dearie, something about ye, now I have caught ye. It is not every day that an old man catches a merry-maid, and I have heard some strange tales of you water-ladies. Now, my dear, don't 'e be afraid, I would not hurt a single hair of that beautiful head. How came ye here?" After some further coaxing she told the old man the following story:—She and her husband and little ones had been busy at sea all the morning, and they were very tired with swimming in the hot sun; so the merman proposed that they should retire to a cavern, which they were in the habit of visiting in Kynance Cove. Away they all swam, and entered the cavern at mid-tide. As there was some nice soft weed, and the cave was deliciously cool, the merman was disposed to sleep, and told them not to wake him until the rise of the tide. He was soon fast asleep, snoring most lustily.

The children crept out and were playing on the lovely sands; so the mermaid thought she should like to look at the world a little. She looked with delight on the children rolling to and fro in the shallow waves, and she laughed heartily at the crabs fighting in their own funny way. "The scent from the flowers came down over the cliffs so sweetly," said she, "that I longed to get nearer the lovely things which yielded those rich odours, and I floated on from rock to rock until I came to this one; and finding that I could not proceed any further, I thought I would seize the opportunity of dressing my hair." She passed her fingers through those beautiful locks, and shook out a number of small crabs, and much broken sea-weed. She went on to say that she had sat on the rock amusing herself, until the voice of a mortal terrified her, and until then she had no idea that the sea was so far out, and a long drybar of sand between her and it. "What shall I do? What shall I do? Oh! I'd give the world to get out to sea! Oh! oh! what shall I do?"

The old man endeavoured to console her; but his attempts were in vain. She told him her husband would "carry on" most dreadfully if he awoke and found her absent, and he would be certain of awaking at the turn of the tide, as that was his dinner-time. He was very savage when he was hungry, and would as soon eat the children as not, if there was no other food at hand. He was also dreadfully jealous, and if she was not at his side when he awoke, he would at once suspect her of having run off with some other merman. She begged the old man to bear her out to sea. If he would but do so, she would procure him any three things he would wish for. Her entreaties at length prevailed; and, according to her desire, the old man knelt down on the rock with his back towards her. She clasped her fair arms around his neck, and locked her long finny fingers together on his throat. He got up from the rock with his burthen, and carried the mermaid thus across the sands. As she rode in this way, she asked the old man to tell her what he desired.

" I will not wish," said he, "for silver and gold, but give me the power to do good to my neighbours: first, to break the spells of witchcraft; next, to charm away diseases; and thirdly, to discover thieves, and restore stolen goods."

All this she promised he should possess; but he must come to a half-tide rock on another day, and she would instruct him how to accomplish the three things he desired. They had reached the water, and taking her comb from her hair, she gave it to the old man, telling him he had but to comb the water and call her at any time, and she would come to him. The mermaid loosened her grasp, and sliding off the old man's back into the sea, she waved him a kiss and disappeared. At the appointed time the old man was at the half-tide rock,—known to the present time as the Mermaid's Rock,—and duly was he instructed in many mysteries. Amongst others, he learned to break the spells of witches from man or beast; to prepare a vessel of water, in which to show to any one who had property stolen the face of the thief; to charm shingles, tetters, St Antony's fire, and St Vitus's dance.

The mermaid had a woman's curiosity, and she persuaded her old friend to take her to some secret place, from which she could see more of the dry land, and of the funny people who lived on it, "and had their tails split, so that they could walk". On taking the mermaid back to the sea, she wished her friend to visit her abode, and promised even to make him young if he would do so, which favour the old gentleman respectfully declined. A family well known in Cornwall, have for some generations exercised the power of charming, &c. They account for the possession of this power in the manner related. Some remote great-grandfather was the individual who received the mermaid's comb, which they retain to the present day, and show us evidence of the truth of their being supernaturally endowed. Some people are unbelieving enough to say the comb is only a part of a shark's jaw.

THE CRICK STONE IN MORVA

IF ANY ONE suffering from a "crick in the back" can pass through this forked rock, on the borders of Zennor and Morva, without touching the stone, he is certain of being cured. This is but a substitute for the holed stone, which, it is admitted, has much more virtue than the forked stone.

In various parts of the county there are, amongst the granitic masses, rocks which have fallen across each other, leaving small openings, or there are holes, low and narrow, extending under a pile of rocks. In nearly every case of this kind, we find it is popularly stated, that any one suffering from rheumatism or lumbago would be cured if he crawled through the openings. In some cases, nine times are insisted on "to make the charm complete".

Mrs Bray, in her "Traditions of Devonshire," gives several examples of the prevalence of this superstition over the granitic district of Dartmoor.

THE MEN-AN-TOL

NOT MORE than two miles from Penzance stands the celebrated cromlech of Lanyon—often pronounced Lanine. This, like all the other cromlechs, marks, no doubt, the resting-place of a British chieftain, many of whose followers repose within a short distance of this, the principal monument.

Beyond the village of Lanyon, on a "furzy down", stands the Men-an-tol, or the "holed stone". For some purpose—it is in vain to speculate on it now—the bardic priesthood employed this stone, and probably the superstition which attaches to it may indicate its ancient uses.

If scrofulous children are passed *naked* through the Men-an-tol three times, and then drawn on the grass three times *against the sun*, it is felt by the faithful that much has been done towards insuring a speedy cure. Even men and women who have been afflicted with spinal diseases, or who have suffered from scrofulous taint, have been drawn through this magic stone, which all declare still retains its ancient virtues.

If two brass pins are carefully laid across each other on the top edge of this stone, any question put to the rock will be answered, by the pins acquiring, through some unknown agency, a peculiar motion.

THE DANCING STONES, THE HURLERS, &c.

IN MANY parts of Cornwall, we find, more or less perfect, circles of stones, which the learned ascribe to the Druids. Tradition, and the common people, who have faith in all that their fathers have taught them, tell us another tale. These stones are everlasting marks of the Divine displeasure, being maidens or men, who were changed into stone for some wicked profanation of the Sabbath-day. These monuments of impiety are scattered over the county; they are to be found, indeed, to the extremity of *Old* Cornwall, many of those circles being upon Dartmoor. It is not necessary to name them all. Every purpose will be served if the tourist is directed to those which lie more directly in the route which is usually prescribed. In the parish of Burian are the "*Dawns Myin*" or *Men*—the dancing stones—commonly called "The Merry Maidens"; and near them are two granite pillars, named the "Pipers". One Sabbath evening some of the thoughtless maidens of the neighbouring village, instead of attending vespers, strayed into the fields, and two evil spirits, assuming the guise of pipers, began to play some dance tunes. The young people yielded to the temptation; and, forgetting the holy day, commenced dancing. The excitement increased with the exercise, and soon the music and the dance became extremely wild; when, lo! a flash of lightning from the clear sky transfixed them all, the tempters and the tempted, and there in stone they stand.

The celebrated circle of nineteen stones,—which is seen on the road to Land's End,—known as the "Boscawen-un Circle," is another example. The "Nine Maids," or the "Virgin Sisters," in Stithians, and other "Nine Maids," or, as called in Cornish, Naw-whoors, in St Columb-Major parish, should also be seen, in the hope of impressing the moral lesson they convey yet more strongly on the mind.

The three circles, which are seen on the moors not far from the

Cheesewring, in the parish of St Cleer, are also notable examples of the punishment of Sabbath-breaking. These are called the "Hurlers," and they preserve the position in which the several parties stood in the full excitement of the game of hurling, when, for the crime of profaning the Sabbath, they were changed into stone.

CUDDEN POINT AND THE SILVER TABLE

THIS POINT is situated in the parish of Perranuthnoe: the parish, it will be remembered, into which Trelawney escaped, aided by the fleetness of his horse, from the deluge which buried the lands between this and the Scilly Isles.

At the low-water of spring tides, the children from all the neighbourhood flock to the sands around this point, in the hope of finding treasure, which they believe is buried in the sands beneath the sea, and which is, it is said, occasionally discovered. Amongst other things, an especial search is made for a silver table, which was lost by a very wealthy lord, by some said to be the old Lord Pengerswick, who enriched himself by grinding down the poor. On one occasion, when the calmness of summer, the clearness of the skies, and the tranquillity of the waters invited the luxurious to the enjoyments of the sea, this magnate, with a party of gay and thoughtless friends, was floating in a beautiful boat lazily with the tide, and feasting from numerous luxuries spread on a silver table. Suddenly—no one lived to tell the cause—the boat sank in the calm, transparent waters; and, long after the event, the fishermen would tell of sounds of revelry heard from beneath the waters, and some have said they have seen these wicked ones still seated around the silver table.

GWAVAS LAKE

ON THE western side of the Mount's Bay, between the fishing-towns of Newlyn and Mousehole is the well-known anchoring-place known by the above name. It is not a little curious that any part of the ocean should have been called a lake. Tradition, however, helps us to an explanation. Between the land on the western side of the bay, and St Michael's Mount on the eastern side, there, at one time, extended a forest of beech-trees. Within this forest, on the western side, was a large lake, and on its banks a hermitage. The saint of the lake was celebrated far and near for his holiness, and his small oratory was constantly resorted to by the diseased in body and the afflicted in mind. None ever came in the true spirit who failed to find relief. The prayers of the saint and the waters of the lake removed the severest pains from the limbs and the deepest sorrows from the mind. The young were strengthened and the old revived by their influences. The great flood however, which separated the Islands of Scilly from England, submerged the forest, and destroyed the lands enclosing this lovely and almost holy lake, burying beneath the waters church and houses, and destroying alike the people and the priest. Those who survived this sad catastrophe built a church on the hill and dedicated it to the saint of the lake—or in Cornish, St Pol—modernised into St Paul.

In support of this tradition, we may see, of a fine summer day, when the tide is low and the waters clear, the remains of a forest in the line passing from St Michael's Mount to Gwavas. At neap-tides the author has gathered beech-nuts from the sands below Chyandour, and cut wood from trees embedded in the sand.

THE LOVERS OF PORTHANGWARTHA

THE NAMES of the youth and maiden who fixed the term of the Lover's Cove upon this retired spot have passed from the memory of man. A simple story, however, remains, the mere fragment, without doubt, of a longer and more ancient tale.

The course of love with this humble pair did not run smooth. On one side or the other the parents were decidedly opposed to the intimacy which existed, and by their persecutions, they so far succeeded, that the young man was compelled to emigrate to some far distant land.

In this cove the lovers met for the last time in life, and vowed under the light of the full moon, that living or dead they would meet at the end of three years.

The young woman remained with her friends—the young man went to the Indies. Time passed on, and the three years, which had been years of melancholy to both, were expiring.

One moonlight night, when the sea was tranquil as a mirror, an old crone sat on the edge of the cliff "making her charms". She saw a figure—she was sure it was a spirit, very like the village maiden—descend into the cove, and seat herself upon a rock, around two-thirds of which the light waves were rippling. On this rock sat the maiden, looking anxiously out over the sea, until, from the rising of the tide, she was completely surrounded. The old woman called; but in vain—the maiden was unconscious of any voice. There she sat, and the tide was rising rapidly around her. The old woman, now seeing the danger in which she was, resolved to go down into the cove, and, if possible, awaken the maiden to a sense of her danger. To do this, it was necessary to go round a projecting pile of rocks. While doing this, she lost sight of the object of her interest, and much was her surprise, when she again saw the maiden, to perceive a young sailor by her side, with his arm around her waist. Conceiving that help had arrived, the old woman sat herself down on the slope of the descending path, and resolved patiently to await the arrival of the pair on shore, and then to rate the girl soundly.

She sat watching this loving and lovely pair, lighted as they were on the black rock by a full flood of moonshine. There they sat, and the tide rose and washed around them. Never were boy and girl so mad, and at last the terrified old woman shrieked with excitement. Suddenly they appeared to float off upon the waters. She thought she heard their voices; but there was no sound of terror. Instead of it a tranquil murmuring music, like the voice of doves, singing,—

"I am thine,   In the wave
Thou art mine,   Be the grave
     Beyond control;   Of heart and soul."

Down, down into the sea passed the lovers. Awestruck, the old woman looked on, until, as she said, "At last they turned round, looked me full in the face, smiling like angels, and, kissing each other, sank to rise no more."

They tell us that the body of the young woman was found a day or two after in a neighbouring cove, and that intelligence eventually reached England that the young man had been killed on this very night.

THE CROWZA STONES

ST JUST, from his home in Penwith, being weary of having little to do, except offering prayers for the tinners and fishermen, went on a visit to the hospitable St Keverne, who had fixed his hermitage in a well-selected spot, not far from the Lizard headland. The holy brothers rejoiced together, and in full feeding and deep drinking they pleasantly passed the time. St Just gloried in the goodly chalice from which he drank the richest of wines, and envied St Keverne the possession of a cup of such rare value. Again and again did he pledge St Keverne; their holy bond of brotherhood was to be for ever; Heaven was to witness the purity of their friendship, and to the world they were to become patterns of ecclesiastical love.

The time came when St Just felt he must return to his flock; and repeating over again his vows, and begging St Keverne to return his visit, he departed—St Keverne sending many a blessing after his good brother.

The Saint of the west had not left his brother of the south many hours before the latter missed his cup. Diligent search was made in every corner of his dwelling, but no cup could be found. At length St Keverne could not but feel that he had been robbed of his treasure by his western friend. That one in whom he had placed such confidence—one to whom he had opened his heart, and to whom he had shown the most unstinting hospitality— should have behaved so treacherously, overcame the serenity of the good man. His rage was excessive. After the first burst was over, and reason reasserted her power, St Keverne felt that his wisest course was to pursue the thief, inflict summary punishment on him, and recover his cup. The thought was followed by a firm resolve, and away St Keverne started in pursuit of St Just. Passing over Crowza Down, some of the boulders of "Ironstone" which are scattered over the surface caught his eye, and he whipped a few of these stone pebbles into his pockets, and hastened onward.

When he drew near Tre-men-keverne he spied St Just. St Keverne worked himself up into a boiling rage, and toiled with increased speed up the hill, hallooing to the saintly thief, who pursued his way for some time in the well-assumed quiet of conscious innocence.

Long and loud did St Keverne call on St Just to stop, but the latter was deaf to all calls of the kind—on he went, quickening, however, his pace a little.

At length St Keverne came within a stone's throw of the dissembling culprit, and calling him a thief—adding thereto some of the most choice epithets from his holy vocabulary—taking a stone from his pocket, he let it fly after St Just.

The stone falling heavily by the side of St Just convinced him that he had to deal with an awkward enemy, and that he had best make all the use he could of his legs. He quietly untied the chalice, which he had fastened to his girdle, and let it fall to the ground. Then, still as if unconscious of his follower, he set off to run as fast as his ponderous body would allow his legs to carry him. St Keverne came up to where his cup glistened in the sunshine. He had recovered his treasure, he should get no good out of the false friend, and he was sadly jaded with his long run. Therefore, he took, one by one, the stones from his pockets—he hurled them, fairly aimed, after the retreating culprit, and cursed him as he went.

There the pebbles remained where they fell,—the peculiarity of the stone being in all respects unlike anything around, but being clearly the Crowza stones,—attesting the truth of the legend; and their weights, each one being several hundred pounds, proving the power of the giant saint.

Many have been the attempts made to remove these stones. They are carried away easily enough by day, but they ever return to the spot on which they now repose, at night.

THE SUICIDE'S SPEARMAN

A FAMILY of the name of Spearman has lived in Cornwall for many ages, their native centre having been somewhere between Ludgvan and St Ives.

Years long ago, an unfortunate man, weary of life, destroyed himself; and the rude laws of a remote age, carrying out, as they thought, human punishments even after death, decreed that the body should be buried at the four cross-roads, and quicklime poured on the corpse.

Superstition stepped in, and somewhat changed the order of burial. To prevent the dead man from "walking," and becoming a terror to all his neighbours, the coffin was to be turned upside down, and a spear was to be driven through it and the body, so as to pin it to the ground.

It was with some difficulty that a man could be found to perform this task. At length, however, a blacksmith undertook it. He made the spear; and after the coffin was properly placed, he drove his spear-headed iron bar through it. From that day he was called "the spearman," and his descendants have never lost the name.

In making a new road not many years since, the coffin and spear were found, and removed. From that time several old men and women have declared that the self-murderer "walks the earth".

ST GERMAN'S WELL

THE GOOD St German was, it would appear, sent into Cornwall in the reign of the Emperor Valentinian, mainly to suppress the Pelagian heresy. The inhabitants of the shores of the Tamar had long been schooled into the belief in original sin, and they would not endure its denial from the lips of a stranger. In this they were supported by the monks, who had already a firm footing in the land, and who taught the people implicit obedience to their religious instructors, faith in election, and that all human efforts were unavailing, unless supported by priestly aid. St German was a man with vast powers of endurance. He preached his doctrines of freewill, and of the value of good works, notwithstanding the outcry raised against him. His miracles were of the most remarkable character, and sufficiently impressive to convince a large body of the Cornish people that he was an inspired priest. St German raised a beautiful church, and built a monastic house for the relief of poor people. Yet notwithstanding the example of the pure life of the saint, and his unceasing study to do good, a large section of the priests and the people never ceased to persecute him. To all human endurance there is a limit, and even that of the saint weakened eventually, before the never-ceasing annoyances by which he was hemmed in.

One Sabbath morning the priest attended as usual to his Christian duties, when he was interrupted by a brawl amongst the outrageous people, who had come in from all parts of the country with a determination to drive him from the place of his adoption. The holy man prayed for his persecutors, and he entreated them to calm their angry passions and listen to his healing words. But no words could convey any healing balm to their stormy hearts. At length his brethren, fearing that his life was in danger, begged him to fly, and eventually he left the church by a small door near the altar, while some of the monks endeavoured to tranquillise the people. St German went, a sad man, to the cliffs at the Rame head, and there alone he wept in agony at the failure of his labours. So intense was the soul-suffering of this holy man, that the rocks felt the power of spirit-struggling, and wept with him. The eyes of man, a spiritual creation, dry after the outburst of sorrow, but when the gross forms of matter are compelled to sympathise with spiritual sorrow, they remain for ever under the influence; and from that day the tears of the cliffs have continued to fall, and the Well of St German attests to this day of the saint's agony. The saint was not allowed to remain in concealment long. The crowd of opposing priests and the peasantry were on his track. Hundreds were on the hill, and arming themselves with stones, they descended with shouts, determined to destroy him. St German prayed to God for deliverance, and immediately a rush, as of thunder, was heard upon the hills—a chariot surrounded by flames, and flashing light in all directions, was seen rapidly approaching. The crowd paused, fell back, and the flaming car passed on to where St German knelt. There were two bright angels in the chariot; they lifted the persecuted saint from the ground, and placing him between them, ascended into the air.

"Curse your persecutors," said the angels. The saint cursed them; and from that time all holiness left the church he had built. The saint was borne to other lands, and lived to effect great good. On the rocks the burnt tracts of the chariot wheels were long to be seen, and the Well of Tears still flows.

TREWA, THE HOME OF WITCHES

As we walk from Nancledrea Bottoms towards Zennor we pass Trewa (pronounced *Truee*), which is said to have been the place where at Midsummer all the witches of the west met. Here are the remains of very ancient tin stream works, and these, I was informed, "were the remains of bals which had been worked before the deluge; there was nothing so old anywhere else in Cornwall". Around us, on the hill-sides and up the bottoms, huge boulders of granite are most fantastically scattered. All these rocks sprang from the ground at the call of the giants. At Embla Green we still see the ruins of the Giant's House, but all we know of this Titan is that he was the king. On one side we have the "Giant's Well," and not far off the "Druid's Well," and a little before us is Zennor quoit or cromlech.

From this point the scenery is of the wildest description. The granite cairns are spread around in every direction, and many of those masses are so strangely fashioned by the atmospheric influences ever acting on them, that fancy can readily fashion them into tombs and temples. Rock basins abound on these hills, and of ruined cromlechs there are many. Whatever the local historians may say, local traditions assure us that on Mid-summer Eve all the witches in Penwith gathered here, and that they lit fires on every cromlech, and in every rock basin, until the hills were alive with flame, and renewed their vows to the evil ones from whom they derived their power. Hence, to this day this place is called Burn Downs. Amidst these rock masses there was one pile remarkable amidst all the others for its size, and—being formed of cubical masses—for its square character. This was known as the Witches' Rock, and here it was said they assembled at midnight to carry on their wicked deeds. This rock has been removed, and with it the witches have died; the last real witch in Zennor having passed away, as I have been told, about thirty years since, and with her, some say, the fairies fled. I have, however, many reasons for believing that our little friends have still a few haunts in this locality. There is but one reason why we should regret the disappearance of the Witches' Rock. *Any one touching this rock nine times at midnight was insured against bad luck.*

MADGY FIGGY'S CHAIR

ALL THOSE who have visited the fine piles of rocks in the vicinity of the so-called "St Levan," Land's-End, called Tol-Pedden-Penwith,—and infinitely finer than anything immediately surrounding the most western promontory itself,—cannot have failed to notice the arrangement of cubical masses of granite piled one upon the other, known as the *Chair Ladder.*

This remarkable pile presents to the beat of the Atlantic waves a sheer face of cliff of very considerable height, standing up like a huge basaltic column, or a pillar bulk by the Titans, the horizontal joints representing so many steps in the so-called "Ladder". On the top is placed a stone of somewhat remarkable shape, which is by no great effort of the imagination converted into a chair. There it was that Madgy Figgy, one of the most celebrated of the St Levan and Burian witches, was in the habit of seating herself when she desired to call up to her aid the spirits of the storm. Often has she been seen swinging herself to and fro on this dizzy height when a storm has been coming home upon the shores, and richly-laden vessels have been struggling with the winds. From this spot she poured forth her imprecations on man and beast, and none whom she had offended could escape those withering spells; and from this "chair," which will ever bear her name, Madgy Figgy would always take her flight. Often, starting like some huge bird, mounted on a stem of ragwort, Figgy has headed a band of inferior witches, and gone off rejoicing in their iniquities to Wales or Spain.

This old hag lived in a cottage not far from Raftra, and she and all her gang, which appears to have been a pretty numerous crew, were notorious wreckers. On one occasion, Madgy from her seat of storms lured a Portuguese Indiaman into Perloe Cove, and drowned all the passengers. As they were washed on shore, the bodies were stripped of everything valuable, and buried by Figgy and her husband in the green hollow, which may yet be seen just above Perloe Cove, marking the graves with a rough stone placed at the head of the corpse. The spoils of this occasion must have been large, for all the women were supplied for years with rich dresses, and costly jewels were seen decking the red arms of the girls who laboured in the fields. For a long time gems and gold continued to be found on the sands. Howbeit, amongst the bodies thrown ashore was one of a lady richly dressed, with chains of gold about her. "Rich and rare were the gems she wore," and not only so, but valuable treasure was fastened around her, she evidently hoping, if saved, to secure some of her property. This body, like all the others, was stripped; but Figgy said there was a mark on it which boded them evil, and she would not allow any of the gold or gems to be divided, as it would be sure to bring bad luck if it were separated. A dreadful quarrel ensued, and bloodshed was threatened; but the diabolical old Figgy was more than a match for any of the men, and the power of her impetuous will was superior to them all.

Everything of value, therefore, belonging to this lady was

gathered into a heap, and placed in a chest in Madgy Figgy's hut. They buried the Portuguese lady the same evening; and after dark a light was seen to rise from the grave, pass along the cliffs, and seat itself in Madgy's chair at Tol-Pedden. Then, after some hours, it descended, passed back again, and, entering the cottage, rested upon the chest. This curious phenomenon continued for more than three months,—nightly,—much to the alarm of all but Figgy, who said she knew all about it, and it would be all right in time. One day a strange-looking and strangely-attired man arrived at the cottage. Figgy's man (her husband) was at home alone. To him the stranger addressed himself by signs,—he could not speak English, so he does not appear to have spoken at all,—and expressed a wish to be led to the graves. Away they went, but the foreigner did not appear to require a guide. He at once selected the grave of the lady, and sitting down upon it, he gave vent to his pent-up sorrows. He sent Figgy's man away, and remained there till night, when the light arose from the grave more brilliant than ever, and proceeded directly to the hut, resting as usual on the chest, which was now covered up with old sails, and all kinds of fishermen's lumber.

The foreigner swept these things aside, and opened the chest. He selected everything belonging to the lady, refusing to take any of the other valuables. He rewarded the wreckers with costly gifts, and left them—no one knowing from whence he came nor whither he went. Madgy Figgy was now truly triumphant. "One witch knows another witch, dead or living," she would say, "and the African would have been the death of us if we hadn't kept the treasure, whereas now we have good gifts, and no gainsaying 'em." Some do say they have seen the light in Madgy Figgy's chair since those times.

CORNISH SORCERERS

THE POWERS OF the sorcerer appear to have been passed on from father to son through a long succession of generations.

There are many families—the descendants from the ancient Cornish people—who are even yet supposed to possess remarkable powers of one kind or another. Several families, which have become extinct, are more especially reputed by tradition to have had dealings with the bad spirits, and many of them to have made compacts with the Evil One himself. Amongst the most curious of the stories once told,—I believe they are nearly all forgotten,—are those connected with Pengerswick Castle. A small tower alone remains to note the site of a once famous fortified place. This castle was said to have been occupied, in the time of Henry VIII, by a man who had committed some great crime; but long previous to that period the place was famous for its wickedness.

THE GHOST ON HORSEBACK

Billy —— and John ——, working at Wheal Vor, were in the habit, early in the morning, of calling out a dog or two, kept by the occupier of an adjoining farm, and with them hunt over the Godolphin warren adjoining. One morning, while thus engaged, one of them gave the alarm that a man on horseback was coming down the road. "'Tisn't possible," said the other; "no horse can ever come over that road." "There is a horse, and old Cap'n T. is upon it," replied the first. "Hold thy tongue," rejoined his comrade; "he's dead months ago." "I know that; but 'tis he, sure enough." Both crouched down behind a bush; and my informant, whose father was one of the parties, declared that the appearance of Capt. T., on a black horse, passed noiselessly down the road immediately before them, but without noticing their presence.

THE LADY WITH THE LANTERN

The night was dark and the wind high. The heavy waves rolled round the point of "the Island" into St Ives Bay, as Atlantic waves only can roll. Everything bespoke a storm of no ordinary character. There were no ships in the bay—not a fishing-boat was afloat. The few small trading vessels had run into Hayle for shelter, or had nestled themselves within that very unquiet resting-place, St Ives pier. The fishing-boats were all high and dry on the sands.

Moving over the rocks which run out into the sea from the eastern side of "the Island" was seen a light. It passed over the most rugged ridges, formed by the intrusive greenstone masses, and over the sharp edges of the upturned slate-rocks with apparent ease. Forth and back—to and from—wandered the light.

"Ha!" said an old sailor with a sigh, as he looked out over the sea; "a sad night! a sad night! The Lady and the Lantern is out."

"The Lady and the Lantern," repeated I; "what do you mean?"

"The light out yonder"——

"Is from the lantern of some fisherman looking for something he has lost." interrupted I.

"Never a fisherman nor a 'salt' either would venture there tonight," said the sailor.

"What is it, then?" I curiously inquired.

"Ha'ast never heard of the Lady and the Lantern?" asked a woman who was standing by.

"Never."

Without any preface, she began at once to enlighten me. I am compelled, however, to reduce her rambling story to something like order, and to make her long-drawn tale as concise as possible.

In the year —— there were many wrecks around the coast. It was a melancholy time. For more than a month there had been a succession of storms, each one more severe than the preceding one. At length, one evening, just about dusk, a large ship came suddenly out of the mist. Her position, it was at once discovered, equally by those on board, and by the people on the shore, was perilous beyond hope. The sailors, as soon as they saw how near they were to the shore, made every effort to save the ship, and then prepare for saving themselves. The tempest raged with such fury from the west, that the ship parted her anchors, at the moment her strain came upon them, and she swung round,—her only sail flying into ribbons in the gale—rushing, as it were, eagerly upon her fate. Presently she struck violently upon a sunken rock, and her masts went by the board, the waves sweeping over her, and clearing her decks. Many perished at once, and, as each successive wave urged her onward, others of the hardy and daring seamen were swept into the angry sea.

Notwithstanding the severity of the storm, a boat was manned by the St Ives fishermen, and launched from within the pier. Their perfect knowledge of their work enabled them, by the efforts of willing hearts, anxiously desiring to succour the distressed, to round the pier-head, and to row towards the ship.

These fishermen brought their boat near to the ship. It was impossible to get close to her, and they called to the sailors on board to throw them ropes. This they were enabled to do, and some two or three of the sailors lowered themselves by their aid, and were hauled into the boat.

Then a group appeared on the deck, surrounding and supporting a lady, who held a child in her arms. They were imploring her to give her charge into the strong arms of a man ere they endeavoured to pass her from the ship to the boat.

The lady could not be prevailed on to part with the infant. The ship was fast breaking up, not a moment could be lost. So the lady, holding her child, was lowered into the sea, and eagerly the fishermen drew her through the waves towards the boat.

In her passage, the lady had fainted, and she was taken into the boat without the infant. The child had fallen from her arms, and was lost in the boiling waters.

Many of the crew were saved by these adventurous men, and taken safely into St Ives. Before morning the shore was strewed with fragments of wreck, and the mighty ship had disappeared.

Life returned to the lady; but, finding that her child was gone, it returned without hope, and she speedily closed her eyes in death. In the churchyard they buried her; but, shortly after her burial, a lady was seen to pass over the wall of the churchyard, on to the beach, and walk towards the Island. There she spent hours amidst the rocks, looking for her child, and not finding it, she would sigh deeply and return to her grave. When the nights were tempestuous or very dark, she carried a lantern; but on fine nights she made her search without a light. The Lady and the Lantern have ever been regarded as predictors of disaster on this shore.

THE TINNER OF CHYANNOR

THE VILLAGE OF Trereen, near the Logan Stone, was at one time an important market-town. Here came all the tin-streamers who worked from Penberth to the hills, and to protect the place and the valuable property which was accumulated here, Castle Trereen was built. Here came—or rather into the cove near it came—the Tyrian merchants. They were not allowed to advance beyond the shores, lest they should discover the country from which the tin was brought. But it is not of them that we have now to tell, but of a knot of tinners who came from the low country between Chyannor and Trengothal. These were assembled round the Garrack Zans, which then stood in the centre of the market-place of Trereen. Times had been bad, and they were consulting together what they had better do. The "streams" had failed them, and they believed all the tin was worked out. Some of them had heard that there was tin in "the country a long way off," some miles beyond Market-Jew, but they had but a very dim idea of the place or of the people. One of them, who, though an old man, was more adventurous than any of his comrades, said he would travel there and see what could be done. It was then determined that Tom Trezidder should try his fortune, and the others would wait until he came home again, or sent for them to come to him. This was soon noised about, and all the women, old and young, came to say "Good-bye" to Tom. His parting with his wife was brief but bitter. He bore up well, and with a stout heart started on his adventure. Tom Trezidder arrived at length at a place not far from Goldsithney, and here he found one of the Jew merchants, who farmed the tin ground, and sold the tin at

St Michael's Mount; and the Jew was very anxious to engage so experienced a "streamer" as Tom was. Tom, nothing loath, took service for a year. He was to have just enough to live on, and a share of profits at the year's end. Tom worked diligently, and plenty of tin was the result of his experienced labour. The year expired, and Tom looked for his share of the profits. The Jew contrived to put Tom off, and promised Tom great things if he would stop for another year, and persuaded him to send for some of his old comrades, clenching every argument which he employed with a small piece of advice, "Never leave an old road for a new one".

The other tinners were shy of venturing so far, so that two or three only could be persuaded to leave the West Country. With Tom and with his brethren the year passed by, and at the end he got no money, but only the same piece of advice, "Never leave an old road for a new one." This went on for a third year, when all of them, being naturally tired of this sort of thing, resolved to go home again.

Tom Trezidder was a favourite with his master, and was greatly esteemed for his honesty and industry by his mistress.

When they left she gave Tom a good currant cake to take home to his old woman, and told him to remember the advice, "Never leave an old road for a new one."

The tinners trudged on together until they were on the western side of Penzance. They were weary, and they found that since they had left home a new road had been made over the hills, which saved them a considerable distance—in fact it was a "short cut". On they went. "No," says Tom; "never leave an old road for a new one." They all laughed at him, and trudged on. But Tom kept in the old road along the valley round the hill. When Tom reached the other end of the "short cut" he thought he would rest a bit, and he sat down by the road-side, and ate his *fuggan*. This his mistress had given him, that he might not break his cake until he got home.

He had not sat long when he heard a noise, and, looking up the hill, he saw his comrades, who he thought were miles in advance of him, slowly and sorrowfully descending it. They came at last to where Tom was seated, and a sad tale had they to tell. They had scarcely got into the new road when they were set upon by robbers, who took from them "all their little bit of money," and then beat them because they had no more.

Tom, you may be sure, thought the piece of advice worth something now, as it had saved his bacon.

Tom arrived home at last, and glad was the old woman to see her old man once again; so she made him some "herby tea" at once. He showed his wife the cake, and told her that all he had received for his share of profits was the piece of advice already given.

The ladies who read this story will understand how vexed was Tom's wife,—there are but few of them who would not have done as she did, that was to seize the cake from the table and fling it at her husband's head, calling him an old fool. Tom Trezidder stooped to avoid the blow. Slap against the corner of the dresser went the cake, breaking in pieces with the blow, and out on the lime-ash floor rolled a lot of gold coins.

This soon changed the aspect of things; the storm rolled back, and sunshine was once more in the cottage. The coins were all gathered up, and they found a scrap of paper, on which, when they got the priest to read it, they discovered was written an exact account of each year's profits, and Tom's share. The three years' shares had been duly hoarded for him by his master and mistress; and now this old couple found they had enough to make them comfortable for the rest of their days. Many were the prayers said by Tom and his wife for the happiness and health of the honest Jew tin merchant and his wife.

THE FAIRY FUNERAL

THE PARISH church of Lelant is curiously situated amidst hills of blown sand, near the entrance of the creek of Hayle. The sandy waste around the church is called the Towen; and this place was long the scene of the midnight gambols of the Small

People. In the adjoining village—or, as it is called in Cornwall, the "church-town"—lived an old woman who had been, according to her own statement, a frequent witness to the use made by the fairies of the Towen. Her husband, also, had seen some extraordinary scenes on the same spot. From her—to me, oft-repeated description—I get the following tale:—It was the fishing season; and Richard had been to St Ives for some fish. He was returning, laden with pilchards, on a beautiful moonlight night; and, as he ascended the hill from St Ives, he thought he heard the bell of Lelant church tolling. Upon a nearer approach, he saw lights in the church; and most distinctly did the bell toll—not with its usual clear sound, but dull and heavy, as if it had been muffled, scarcely awakening any echo. Richard walked towards the church, and cautiously, but not without fear, approaching one of the windows, looked in. At first he could not perceive any one within, nor discover whence the light came by which everything was so distinctly illuminated. At length he saw, moving along the centre aisle, a funeral procession. The little people who crowded the aisle, although they all looked very sorrowful, were not dressed in any mourning garments—so far from it, they wore wreaths of little roses, and carried branches of the blossoming myrtle. Richard beheld the bier borne between six—whether men or women he could not tell—but he saw that the face of the corpse was that of a beautiful female, smaller than the smallest child's doll. It was, Richard said, "as if it were a dead seraph,"—so very lovely did it appear to him. The body was covered with white flowers, and its hair, like gold threads, was tangled amongst the blossoms. The body was placed within the altar; and then a large party of men, with picks and spades, began to dig a little hole close by the sacramental table. Their task being completed, others, with great care, removed the body and placed it in the hole. The entire company crowded around, eager to catch a parting glimpse of that beautiful corpse, ere yet it was placed in the earth. As it was lowered into the ground, they began to tear off their flowers and break their branches of myrtle, crying, "Our queen is dead! our queen is dead!" At length one of the men who had dug the grave threw a shovelful of earth upon the body; and the shriek of the fairy host so alarmed Richard, that he involuntarily joined in it. In a moment, all the lights were extinguished, and the fairies were heard flying in great consternation in every direction. Many of them brushed past the terrified man, and, shrieking, pierced him with sharp instruments. He was compelled to save his life *by the most rapid flight.*